WHEN SILENCE SPEAKS LOUDER

*Finding God's Purpose in Rejection, Betrayal,
Persecution, and Accusations*

PETER LENGWE

Printed in the United States of America

ISBN:
Softcover: 978-1-972299-27-2
Hardback   978-1-972299-28-9
eBook: 978-1-972299-26-5

For permission requests, visit and write to the publisher at:

Peter Lengwe | THE BREAD OF LIFE GLOBAL MINISTRIES

DEDICATION

To my Lord and Savior Jesus Christ,

the One who was despised and rejected for my sake,

yet who turned silence into salvation, scars into glory,

and rejection into redemption.

And to every brother and sister who has walked through

rejection, betrayal, false accusation, and silence—

this book is for you.

May you discover that your pain is not the end,

but the very platform God will use to reveal His glory.

INTRODUCTION

R ejection is one of the deepest wounds the human heart can endure. Betrayal cuts even deeper—especially when it comes not from strangers but from those we once trusted, prayed with, or called family in the household of faith. Many carry these wounds silently. They smile in public, but in private they bleed.

I know this pain because I have walked through it. As I was drafting my last book, I was not only wrestling with Scripture and prophecy—I was wrestling with rejection. I felt the sting of being misunderstood, criticized, and even pushed aside by those I thought would support me. The silence of others spoke louder than words, and their absence felt heavier than open hostility.

It is in moments like these that the enemy whispers: "You are not enough. You are not chosen. You are forgotten." But the truth is, rejection often comes right before God's greatest redirection. The very stone that the builders reject becomes the chief cornerstone. Jesus Himself was despised and rejected by men, yet He fulfilled the will of the Father.

In these pages, I want to walk with you through the valley of rejection and betrayal—not to stir bitterness, but to uncover healing. Together we will see how silence, when surrendered to God, becomes louder than accusations. We will learn that what others push away, God embraces. We will discover that rejection does not define you—it refines you.

This book is for every believer who has been wounded in the place they expected love. It is for those who have cried behind closed doors after leaving a church service. It is for the servant of God who gave their all, only to be overlooked. It is for the son or daughter who has carried the pain of abandonment.

I write this not only as a teacher of Scripture but as a fellow traveler who has felt the ache of rejection. And I want you to know: you are not alone, and you are not forgotten. Your silence speaks louder than you realize. God counts your tears. Your rejection is not the end of your story—it may be the very place where God's purpose breaks forth.

As you turn these pages, may the Holy Spirit touch the tender places of your heart. May you hear the voice of the One who was rejected so that you could be accepted. And may you rise from rejection with renewed strength, unshakable identity, and a testimony that speaks louder than words.

CHAPTERS

Part I – The Wound of Rejection

1. When Silence Speaks – Jesus' silence before Pilate, and your personal story.

2. The Ache of Betrayal – Judas, Peter, and David's betrayals.

3. The Hidden Battle of Identity – Jesus in Nazareth, Joseph with his brothers.

Part II – The Silence of the Savior

1. Silent Strength – Jesus' trial and Jeremiah's silencing.

2. The Cornerstone Rejected – Jesus rejected, Moses overlooked.

3. The Voice in the Silence – Elijah's whisper, Hannah's prayer, Jesus in Gethsemane.

Part III – Redemption Through Rejection

1. What Man Rejects, God Selects – Jesus' disciples, Gideon's call.

2. Healing the Wounds of Church Hurt – Jesus cleansing the temple, Paul rejected.

3. From Wounds to Witness – Jesus' scars to Thomas, Joseph's testimony.

Part IV – Living as the Chosen

1. Walking in Prophetic Purpose – Jesus toward Jerusalem, Esther's courage.

2. Silence That Roars – Jesus' silence at the cross, Job's endurance.

3. My Journey Through It All – Your personal story of rejection, obedience, and God's faithfulness.

4. Faith, the Principal Thing – Living by faith, not sight; the foundation of Christian life.

CHAPTER 1
WHEN SILENCE SPEAKS

Rejection does not always shout. Sometimes, it whispers. Sometimes, it hides behind polite smiles, unanswered messages, or the quiet turning away of those we thought we could trust. But if you have ever been rejected, you know that silence can speak louder than the harshest words.

When I faced rejection in the church, it was not always an open confrontation. It was the quiet withdrawal, the avoidance, the subtle looks, the closed doors. It was people I had prayed with and poured into who suddenly pretended I was not there. Silence became its own voice—cold, sharp, and heavy.

And in those moments, I wrestled with questions I could not silence within myself: "Why me, Lord? Did I do something wrong? Am I truly called, or was I mistaken? If even Your people turn away, where do I stand?"

If you have ever sat in a crowded sanctuary but felt invisible… if you have given your best only to be overlooked… if you have been silenced when you longed to speak truth… then you know this pain. You know the kind of silence that cuts deeper than insults.

The Silent Savior

As I cried out to God, He reminded me: Jesus too was met with silence.

He healed multitudes, yet when He stood before Pilate, the voices of those He helped were absent. The same people who shouted "Hosanna!" days earlier were nowhere to be found when the crowd cried out, "Crucify Him!" (Mark 15:13–14). The silence of His friends, the betrayal of Judas, the denial of Peter—these pierced deeper than the nails that held Him to the cross.

Isaiah prophesied of Him:

"He was oppressed and He was afflicted, yet He opened not His mouth.
He was led as a lamb to the slaughter,
and as a sheep before its shearers is silent,
so, He opened not His mouth." (Isaiah 53:7, NKJV)

The Son of God chose silence—not because He was weak, but because He was strong. He understood that sometimes silence is the loudest statement of all.

What Silence Reveals

Rejection has a way of revealing what we rely on. When people turn away, we discover whether our identity rests on their approval or on God's acceptance. When voices fade, we are left to hear the only voice that truly matters—the still, small voice of the Holy Spirit.

I began to realize that silence was not the end of my story—it was the beginning of God speaking in a new way. When others refused to affirm me, God whispered: "I chose you before the foundation of the world. I have not rejected you."

In your silence, God is still speaking. In your rejection, God is still choosing.

Reflection

- Where have you felt the sting of silence?

- Did it come from family, friends, or even fellow believers?

- How did that silence make you question your worth?

Take these questions to prayer. Print the names, the moments, the wounds. Bring them before the Lord who knows rejection Himself.

Prayer

Father, I lay before You the silence that has wounded me. I confess the pain of being rejected, overlooked, or abandoned. But I thank You that when others turned away, you turned toward me. Heal my heart, Lord. Teach me to hear Your voice above the silence of men. Remind me that I am chosen, accepted, and loved in You. In Jesus' name, amen.

Chapter 2
The Ache of Betrayal

Rejection hurts—but betrayal feels like a knife to the soul. Rejection can come from the outside, but betrayal usually comes from the inside. It comes from the people we trusted most. And that is why its ache lingers longer than almost any other wound.

When strangers dismiss us, we can brush it off. But when it's a friend who prayed with you, walked with you, and broke bread with you—yet turns their back—that pain is almost unbearable. Scripture says it clearly:

"Even my own familiar friend in whom I trusted,
Who ate my bread,
Has lifted up his heel against me."
(Psalm 41:9, NKJV)

Judas: Betrayed With a Kiss

The most painful betrayal in history came with an act of affection. Judas walked closely with Jesus for three years. He saw miracles, heard teaching, and sat at the same table. Yet in the garden, with soldiers surrounding, Judas betrayed Him with a kiss (Luke 22:48).

The kiss was supposed to mark intimacy, loyalty, and brotherhood. But in Judas' lips was deception. What looked like love was the dagger of betrayal.

And yet—Jesus did not resist. He called Judas "friend" even in that moment (Matthew 26:50). The Lamb of God absorbed the sting of betrayal, not with bitterness, but with submission to the Father's plan. Because He knew that betrayal was not the end—it was the pathway to the cross, and the cross was the doorway to resurrection.

Peter: The Pain of Denial

It wasn't just Judas. Peter, the one who swore, "I will never leave You," denied Him three times before the rooster crowed (Luke 22:61). Jesus heard the words of denial from the lips of His closest disciple. And when their eyes met, Peter wept bitterly.

The silence of those who fled, the betrayal of Judas, the denial of Peter—these wounds pierced deeper than the nails. Jesus bore them all. He understands the ache of betrayal more than anyone.

David: Betrayed by His Own

Long before Christ walked the earth, David endured betrayal that mirrored the pain of Jesus. His own son Absalom rose against him, and Ahithophel—his trusted counselor—turned to side with the enemy (2 Samuel 15–16).

The grief broke David. He cried out in the Psalms about the torment of betrayal:

"For it is not an enemy who reproaches me;
Then I could bear it.
Nor is it one who hates me who has exalted himself against me;

Then I could hide from him.
But it was you, a man my equal,
My companion and my acquaintance."
(Psalm 55:12–13, NKJV)

Like Jesus, David's greatest wound came not from his enemies, but from those closest to him.

God's Redemption Through Betrayal

But here is the mystery of God's plan: betrayal is often the stage for elevation.

- Judas' kiss led Jesus to the cross, where redemption for the world was bought.

- Peter's denial was restored by three affirmations of love, making him a pillar of the early church.

- David's betrayal led to his deeper dependence on God, preparing him for greater kingship.

What Satan meant for destruction, God turned into destiny. Betrayal became the very place where God's purpose was revealed.

For You, Reader...

You too have been betrayed—by a friend, a church leader, a family member. Maybe you've cried, "Lord, not them. Anyone but them." The ache is real. The wound is deep. But you must know: God is not finished.

Betrayal is not where your story ends. In the hands of God, it is the doorway to your greatest testimony. What others meant for harm, God will use for good.

Reflection

- Who has betrayed you, and what wound has it left behind?

- How has betrayal shaken your trust—in people, and even in God?

- Can you believe that God can turn even this pain into purpose?

Prayer

Father, you know the ache of betrayal. You saw Judas kiss Your Son. You heard Peter's denial. You felt David's cry. And You see my pain too. Today, I lay before You the wounds of betrayal. I ask for healing where the knife cut deep. I choose to trust You, Lord—that You can take this pain and turn it for my elevation. Give me the grace to forgive, and the faith to believe that betrayal is not my end, but the beginning of something greater. In Jesus' name, amen.

CHAPTER 3
THE HIDDEN BATTLE OF IDENTITY

Rejection doesn't only wound our hearts—it often strikes at the very core of who we are. It makes us question our value, our calling, and even our place in God's plan.

When people ignore you, criticize you, or turn away from you, the enemy takes advantage. He whispers lies: "You are not chosen. You are not called. You are not enough." And if we are not careful, those lies can begin to shape our identity.

But rejection never has the final word. God does.

Jesus Rejected in His Hometown

Even Jesus, the Son of God, faced rejection where He least expected it—among His own people. When He returned to Nazareth, the place where He grew up, He preached in the synagogue with wisdom and authority. But instead of embracing Him, His neighbors scoffed:

"Is this not the carpenter, the Son of Mary…?
And they were offended at Him."
(Mark 6:3, NKJV)

They could not see beyond His ordinary beginnings. To them, He was still the carpenter's son, not the Messiah. The Bible says:

"A prophet is not without honor except in his own country, among his own relatives, and in his own house."
(Mark 6:4, NKJV)

The rejection in Nazareth was not about His miracles or His teaching—it was about His identity. They reduced Him to what they thought they knew, and because of their unbelief, Jesus could do few mighty works there.

Rejection looks to confine you to the past, to keep you small, to strip you of your God-given identity. But like Jesus, you cannot allow man's perception to define God's truth about you.

Joseph: Rejected by His Brothers

Joseph dreamed dreams of greatness. He saw visions of leadership and divine purpose. But the very ones who should have celebrated him—his brothers—hated him for it. They stripped him of his coat, threw him into a pit, and sold him into slavery (Genesis 37:23–28).

What was their reason? Jealousy. His dreams and his favor from the Father made them uncomfortable. They said in mockery:

"Look, this dreamer is coming! Come therefore, let us now kill him and cast him into some pit…"
(Genesis 37:19–20, NKJV)

Joseph's rejection was not about his coat—it was about his calling. The enemy looked to destroy his identity before it could fully manifest. Yet in Egypt, in prison, and in the palace, Joseph held on to God's Word. And in the end, the very rejection that looked to bury him became the vehicle that carried him to the throne.

The Battle for Identity

Rejection will always raise the same question: "Who are you really?"

- To Jesus, they said: "Isn't this just the carpenter?"

- To Joseph, they said: "Here comes the dreamer—let's silence him."

- To you, rejection may say: "You are not qualified. You are not wanted. You are not called."

But here is the truth:

- Jesus was not "just the carpenter." He was the Christ, the Son of the Living God.

- Joseph was not "just a dreamer." He was destined to save nations.

- And you are not what rejection labels you. You are who God says you are chosen, called, beloved.

God's Declaration Over You

Before anyone accepted or rejected you, God had already spoken. He said:

"...He chose us in Him before the foundation of the world, that we should be holy and without blame before Him in love."
(Ephesians 1:4, NKJV)

Your identity is not built on people's acceptance—it is anchored in God's choosing.

Reflection

- Has rejection ever made you question your worth or calling?

- Who has tried to reduce you to your past or your limitations?

- How can you begin to see yourself as God sees you, not as man labels you?

Prayer

Father, I confess that rejection has sometimes made me doubt who I am in You. I've allowed man's words to weigh heavier than Your Word. But today, I break free from those lies. I declare that I am chosen, loved, and called by You. Lord, let me walk in the identity You have spoken over me since before the foundation of the world. In Jesus' name, amen.

CHAPTER 4
JESUS AND THE SILENT STRENGTH

Silence can be misunderstood. To the world, silence looks like weakness, like defeat, like surrender. But in God's hands, silence is not weakness—it is strength. It is restraint. It is trust. It is the refusal to fight battles that belong to the Lord.

When Jesus stood trial before Pilate, He faced false accusations, lies, and slander. The religious leaders stirred the crowd against Him, twisting His words and mocking His mission. Yet the Gospels tell us:

"But He kept silent and answered nothing."
(Mark 14:61, NKJV)

Pilate was astonished. Most men would have fought back, defended themselves, or begged for mercy. But Jesus remained silent. His silence spoke louder than their accusations. His silence declared: "I am not here to save Myself. I am here to fulfill the will of My Father."

Silence as Prophecy Fulfilled

Isaiah had already seen this moment centuries earlier:

"He was oppressed and He was afflicted,
Yet He opened not His mouth.
He was led as a lamb to the slaughter,
And as a sheep before its shearers is silent,
So He opened not His mouth."
(Isaiah 53:7, NKJV)

Jesus' silence was not a failure to respond—it was prophecy fulfilled. In His silence, He declared that He was the Lamb of God, willingly laying down His life for the sins of the world.

Jeremiah: Silenced but Not Defeated

Jesus was not the first prophet to face rejection and silence. Jeremiah, known as the "weeping prophet," was despised for his message. He warned Judah of coming judgment, but the people mocked him, beat him, and threw him into a cistern of mud (Jeremiah 38:6).

Jeremiah reached a breaking point. He cried out:

"Then I said, 'I will not make mention of Him,
Nor speak anymore in His name.'
But His word was in my heart like a burning fire
Shut up in my bones;
I was weary of holding it back,
And I could not."
(Jeremiah 20:9, NKJV)

Even when silenced by rejection, Jeremiah's calling burned too deeply to be extinguished. His silence, like Jesus', was not weakness—it became strength, for it drove him deeper into God's fire within.

Strength in Restraint

Silence needs greater strength than speaking.

- Anyone can lash out.

- Anyone can defend themselves with anger.

- But it takes God-given strength to remain silent when falsely accused, mocked, or rejected.

Jesus could have called down legions of angels to His defense (Matthew 26:53). Jeremiah could have walked away from his calling. But both chose restraint. They chose to trust the Father's plan more than their own vindication.

And that is the strength we are called to walk in too.

For You, Reader...

When people lie about you, when they twist your words, when they misunderstand your heart—you will face the temptation to defend yourself, to fight back, to prove them wrong. But sometimes God calls you to be silent. Not because you are weak, but because your silence declares: "The Lord is my Defender."

In silence, you trust that God sees, God knows, and God will vindicate in His time.

Reflection

- Have you ever been accused or misunderstood but chose silence instead of defense?

- Did your silence feel like weakness, or did you sense God's strength in it?

- How can you trust God to be your Defender in situations where words won't help ?

Prayer

Father, give me the strength to be silent when silence speaks louder than words. Teach me to trust You as my Defender. When I am accused or rejected, remind me of Jesus' silence before Pilate and Jeremiah's fire shut up in his bones. May my silence not be weakness, but strength that declares my confidence in You. In Jesus' name, amen.

CHAPTER 5
THE CORNERSTONE REJECTED

Rejection does not end God's plan—it reveals it. What man discards, God often chooses. What people push aside, God places at the center.

The psalmist declared a mystery that would be fulfilled in Christ:

"The stone which the builders rejected
Has become the chief cornerstone.
This was the Lord's doing;
It is marvelous in our eyes."
(Psalm 118:22–23, NKJV)

The builders thought the stone was useless, out of place, unfit for their structure. But God took the rejected stone and made it the foundation of everything.

Jesus: The Rejected Stone

Jesus came as the Messiah, the fulfillment of prophecy, the very Word made flesh. Yet He was despised and rejected. The leaders of Israel—the "builders" of the religious system—examined Him and found no place for Him in their plans.

- They said He was a blasphemer.

- They mocked His miracles.

- They rejected His kingship.

But God exalted Him. The One they crucified became the Savior of the world. The stone they cast aside became the cornerstone of a new covenant; a living temple not made with hands.

Peter, who once denied Jesus, later stood before the rulers and boldly proclaimed:

"This is the 'stone, which was rejected by you builders, which has become the chief cornerstone.' Nor is there salvation in any other, for there is no other name under heaven given among men by which we must be saved."
(Acts 4:11–12, NKJV)

What they rejected became the very thing they needed most.

Moses: Rejected Yet Raised Up

Long before Christ, another deliverer faced rejection. Moses, called by God to rescue Israel, first tried to act in his own strength. When he killed an Egyptian taskmaster, his own people turned on him:

"Who made you a prince and a judge over us?"
(Exodus 2:14, NKJV)

Rejected by his own, Moses fled into the wilderness. For forty years, he lived hidden, forgotten by men—but not by God. When the time was right, the very people who once rejected him were delivered by his hand, under God's power.

The rejection Moses faced was not the end—it was the preparation. God used the wilderness to shape him into the deliverer Israel needed.

The Pattern of God

There is a pattern throughout Scripture:

- Joseph was rejected by his brothers but became a ruler in Egypt.

- David was overlooked by his father and despised by Saul but became king.

- Moses was rejected by his people but returned as their deliverer.

- Jesus was despised by the builders but became the Cornerstone.

Rejection is not evidence of your disqualification—it is often confirmation of your calling.

For You, Reader…

If you feel like the stone the builders have cast aside, take heart. God is not finished. The rejection you face today may be the very thing that positions you for tomorrow's elevation.

You may have been overlooked, pushed aside, or told you are not fit—but God specializes in choosing the rejected and making them the foundation of His work.

Reflection

- Where have you felt like a "rejected stone"?

- Who has dismissed or overlooked the calling God placed on your life?

- Can you believe that your rejection may be God's preparation for elevation?

Prayer

Father, thank You that rejection does not define me—Your calling does. Just as Jesus became the cornerstone and Moses was raised up as deliverer, I believe you can take my rejection and turn it into elevation. Help me to trust You're timing and Your plan, even when others cannot see my worth. In Jesus' name, amen.

Chapter 6
The Voice in the Silence

Rejection and betrayal can leave us surrounded by silence—the silence of absent friends, unanswered questions, and the emptiness that follows broken trust. But silence is not always an enemy. In fact, silence is often the very place where God's voice is heard most clearly.

Elijah: The Whisper on the Mountain

The prophet Elijah knew rejection well. After his great victory over the prophets of Baal, Queen Jezebel threatened his life. Afraid and worn down, Elijah fled into the wilderness, sat under a broom tree, and prayed to die. "It is enough! Now, Lord, take my life." (1 Kings 19:4, NKJV).

Lonely, exhausted, and rejected by his people, Elijah felt like a failure. He believed he was all alone. But God drew him to Mount Horeb, where He would teach Elijah how He truly works.

The Bible tells us:

"And behold, the Lord passed by, and a great and strong wind tore into the mountains… but the Lord was not in the wind; and after the wind an earthquake, but the Lord was not in the earthquake; and after the earthquake a fire, but the Lord was not in the fire; and after the fire a still small voice."
(1 Kings 19:11–12, NKJV)

God was not in the noise, the shaking, or the fire. He was in the whisper.

In the silence, Elijah discovered the power of God's gentle voice. The prophet who felt abandoned realized he was not alone. The whisper carried God's reassurance: "You are not finished. I still have purpose for you."

Hannah: A Silent Prayer That Changed History

Hannah also knew the pain of rejection. She longed for a child, yet was barren, mocked by her rival, and misunderstood even by her husband. Year after year, her prayers seemed unanswered.

One day, in her deep distress, Hannah poured out her soul before the Lord—not with words men could hear, but in silent anguish.

"Now Hannah spoke in her heart; only her lips moved, but her voice was not heard."
(1 Samuel 1:13, NKJV)

Even the priest Eli mistook her for being drunk. But God heard the prayer no one else could. And in time, Hannah conceived and bore Samuel, one of the greatest prophets in Israel's history.

Her silent prayer shook heaven, even when men misunderstood it.

Jesus: Hearing the Father in Silence

Jesus too lived in constant communion with His Father, often withdrawing to lonely places to pray in silence (Luke 5:16). On the night of His betrayal, He knelt in Gethsemane. While His disciples slept, the

Son poured out His heart in silence broken only by tears and sweat like drops of blood (Luke 22:44).

Even when heaven seemed quiet, Jesus trusted the Father's will: "Not My will, but Yours, be done." His strength came not from noise or applause, but from the silent place of surrender.

Learning to Hear in Silence

God does not always answer in the way we expect. We often look for the dramatic—the earthquake, the fire, the signs that shake the earth. But more often, His voice comes in stillness, in quietness, in the whisper that only the surrendered heart can hear.

Silence does not mean God is absent. Silence is often His invitation to lean in closer.

For You, Reader...

Perhaps you've been wounded by rejection and all you hear now is silence. The calls stopped. The support ended. The prayers of others faded. But do not mistake the silence for God's absence. In the quiet, He is whispering. In the stillness, He is near.

Like Elijah, He is saying: "You are not alone."

Like Hannah, He is saying: "Your prayer is heard."

Like Jesus, He is saying: "Trust My will."

Reflection

- When has God seemed silent in your life?

- Have you ever mistaken His silence for abandonment?

- What "whispers" of His presence or direction have you overlooked in the quiet?

Prayer

Father, teach me to hear Your voice in the silence. When others turn away and the noise fades, open my ears to Your whisper. Let me find strength, like Elijah, in Your gentle voice. Let my silent prayers, like Hannah's, reach Your throne. And let me, like Jesus, trust Your will even in the quiet. In Jesus' name, amen.

CHAPTER 7
WHAT MAN REJECTS, GOD SELECTS

The world has a system of value. It celebrates strength, status, and success. It elevates the eloquent, the powerful, and the wealthy. But God's ways are not man's ways. Repeatedly, Scripture reveals a divine pattern: the ones men reject, God selects.

Jesus: Choosing the Outcasts

When Jesus began His ministry, He did not choose the religious elite or the well-educated scribes. He walked past the polished halls of Jerusalem's teachers and instead called fishermen from Galilee.

- Peter, Andrew, James, and John were ordinary laborers with no rabbinical training.

- Matthew was a despised tax collector, hated by his own people.

- Simon the Zealot had been a revolutionary.

- Even Judas was not chosen because of his purity, but because prophecy had to be fulfilled.

The Pharisees sneered at Jesus for eating with sinners and tax collectors. But He answered:

"Those who are well have no need of a physician, but those who are sick. I did not come to call the righteous, but sinners, to repentance."
(Mark 2:17, NKJV)

The very one's society dismissed as unworthy became the foundation of the Church. The rejected became His chosen.

Gideon: From Hiding to Hero

Generations earlier, the Midianites oppressed Israel. Into this despair, God called Gideon. But when the angel of the Lord appeared, Gideon was not leading an army—he was hiding in a winepress, threshing wheat in secret (Judges 6:11).

The angel declared:

"The Lord is with you, you mighty man of valor!"
(Judges 6:12, NKJV)

Gideon could hardly believe it. He protested: "My clan is the weakest in Manasseh, and I am the least in my father's house." (Judges 6:15, NKJV). In other words: "I am rejected, overlooked, insignificant."

But God saw something different. He saw not Gideon's weakness, but His own strength working through Gideon. And the man the world overlooked became the leader God used to deliver Israel with just three hundred men.

God's Pattern of Selection

This is God's way:

- David was the forgotten shepherd boy, but God made him king.

- Joseph was the despised dreamer, but God set him over nations.

- Moses was the fugitive in the wilderness, but God called him to deliver His people.

- The disciples were ordinary men, but God used them to change the world.

Man looks at the outward appearance. God looks at the heart (1 Samuel 16:7).

For You, Reader...

Maybe you feel disqualified. Rejection has convinced you that you are not worthy to be used by God. But take courage: the very things that disqualify you in the eyes of men may be the things God uses to qualify you in His kingdom.

When man says, "Not you," God says, "Yes, you."

When man says, "You're too weak," God says, "My strength is made perfect in weakness."

When man says, "You're not enough," God says, "You are chosen, beloved, and appointed."

Reflection

- Who has dismissed you as unworthy or unqualified?

- In what ways have you believed man's rejection over God's Selection ?

- How might God be positioning you, even now, for something greater?

Prayer

Father, thank You that You do not choose as men choose. Thank You for selecting the rejected, the overlooked, and the broken. Lord, I surrender my feelings of unworthiness to You. Use me, like Gideon, like the disciples, like David—not because of my strength, but because of Yours. Remind me that I am chosen and let me walk boldly in that calling. In Jesus' name, amen.

Chapter 8
Healing the Wounds of Church Hurt

S ome of the deepest wounds do not come from the world—they come from within the walls of the church. The place we expected to find love; we sometimes find rejection. The place we thought would be a refuge, sometimes becomes a battlefield.

If you have ever walked away from a church service with tears not from conviction but from pain, you know the weight of church hurt. You know the sting of being silenced, overlooked, or betrayed by those who carry the name of Christ.

But I want you to know this: Jesus understands. He, too, faced rejection from the very house of God. And He carries healing for every wound the church has left on your heart.

Jesus Cleansing the Temple

When Jesus entered the temple courts, He did not find the holiness of His Father's house. Instead, He found corruption—money changers turning worship into profit, priests exploiting the poor. And with righteous anger, He drove them out, declaring:

"It is written, 'My house shall be called a house of prayer,' but you have made it a 'den of thieves.'"
(Matthew 21:13, NKJV)

The temple—the very center of worship—had become a place of exploitation. If Jesus Himself was grieved by what happened in God's house, should we be surprised when we feel the sting of corruption, hypocrisy, or abuse within modern churches?

Yet notice this: Jesus did not turn His back on the Father's house altogether. He cleansed it. He restored it to its true purpose. This shows us that while church hurt is real, God's design for His Church is still holy, still pure, and still His bride.

Paul: Rejected by His Own

Paul, once a Pharisee, devoted his life to preaching Christ. Yet everywhere he went, he faced rejection—especially from his own people. In Acts 13, after boldly preaching in Antioch, the Jews stirred up persecution against him and drove him out.

Paul's response was firm but faith-filled:

"It was necessary that the word of God should be spoken to you first; but since you reject it, and judge yourselves unworthy of everlasting life, behold, we turn to the Gentiles."
(Acts 13:46, NKJV)

Paul did not deny the pain of rejection, but he did not let it paralyze him either. He released those who rejected him and turned to those who were ready to receive. That's a lesson for us: sometimes healing begins when we release those who hurt us and step into the new doors God is opening.

The Pain and the Healing

Church hurt is real. It can leave scars that make us hesitant to trust again, afraid to serve again, or even tempted to walk away from God altogether. But we must remember:

- The Church belongs to Christ, not to man.

- People may fail us, but Jesus never will.

- What was misused in man's hands, God can restore in His.

Healing begins when we bring our wounds to the One who bore the ultimate rejection. Jesus was despised and rejected so that in Him, we might be healed and accepted forever.

For You, Reader…

If you carry the weight of church hurt, know this: God sees your pain. The betrayal, the misunderstanding, the silencing—it is not hidden from Him. And He is not only your Healer, but the One who can redeem even this pain for His glory.

Reflection

- Have you ever been wounded within the church? How did it affect your faith?

- Have you mistaken the failures of people for the failure of God?

- What might it look like for you to release those who hurt you into God's hands and step forward in healing?

Prayer

Father, I bring before You the wounds I have carried from Your house. I confess the bitterness, the hurt, and the disappointment. But today, I choose to release those who hurt me into Your hands. Heal my heart, Lord. Restore my trust in You and remind me that Your Church is still Your bride.

Help me to love Your house as You do, and to walk in freedom from the pain of the past. In Jesus' name, amen.

Chapter 9
From Wounds to Witness

Wounds hurt. They bleed, they ache, and they leave scars. But when wounds are surrendered to God, they do not remain places of shame—they become testimonies of grace. What once caused us to hide can become the very thing that helps others find healing.

Jesus: Showing His Scars

After the resurrection, Jesus appeared to His disciples. But Thomas was not present the first time, and he refused to believe unless he saw for himself. "Unless I see in His hands the print of the nails and put my finger into the print of the nails, and put my hand into His side, I will not believe." (John 20:25, NKJV).

Eight days later, Jesus appeared again. This time, He turned to Thomas and invited him to touch His scars:

"Reach your finger here, and look at My hands; and reach your hand

here, and put it into My side. Do not be unbelieving, but believing."
(John 20:27, NKJV)

The risen Savior still bores the marks of crucifixion. He could have risen without scars, but He chose to keep them. Why? Because His wounds were now His witness. They testified that death had been conquered, that the price had been paid, that love had triumphed.

Your scars, too, can testify. The things you thought would destroy you can become the very proof that God has delivered you.

Joseph: Redeeming His Betrayal

Joseph's life was marked by wounds of betrayal. Sold into slavery by his brothers, falsely accused in Egypt, forgotten in prison—his scars ran deep. Yet when God raised him to power in Egypt and his brothers stood before him, fearful for their lives, Joseph declared one of the most powerful truths in all of Scripture:

"But as for you, you meant evil against me; but God meant it for good, in order to bring it about as it is this day, to save many people alive."
(Genesis 50:20, NKJV)

Joseph did not deny the evil that was done. He did not pretend the betrayal never happened. Instead, he reframed it: the wound became a witness of God's redemptive power. What was meant to bury him became the very thing that positioned him to save nations.

Scars as Testimonies

We often want to hide our wounds. But God calls us to show our scars because scars are no longer bleeding—they are healed. They tell the story of pain endured, but also of grace received.

- Your story of rejection can become someone else's hope.

- Your testimony of betrayal can help another believer endure.

- Your scars can speak louder than sermons because they prove that God heals, restores, and redeems.

For You, Reader...

What scars do you carry? What wounds still ache when touched? Do not despise them. Do not hide them in shame. When placed in God's hands, they become your witness.

You may one day stand before someone who is doubting, like Thomas, or broken, like Joseph's brothers—and your story will help them believe.

Reflection

- What wounds in your life has God already begun to turn into testimonies?

- Are there scars you have been hiding out of shame that God wants to use as witness?

- Who in your life might need to see your scars so they can believe in God's healing?

Prayer

Father, thank You that my wounds are not wasted. Thank You that what the enemy meant for evil, you turn for good. Lord, help me not to hide my scars, but to use them as a witness of Your power and grace. Just as Jesus showed His wounds to Thomas, let my life testify that You are real, that You heal, and that You redeem. In Jesus' name, amen.

CHAPTER 10
CHOSEN, NOT FORSAKEN

Rejection can make us feel abandoned, forgotten, and cast aside. But while people may turn away, God never does. His choosing is eternal, His love unshakable, and His calling irrevocable.

When man says, "You're not enough," God declares, "You are Mine."

Jesus: Affirmed by the Father

Before Jesus performed a single miracle, preached a sermon, or healed the sick, the Father publicly declared His approval. At His baptism, as He came up out of the water, the heavens opened, and a voice spoke:

"This is My beloved Son, in whom I am well pleased."
(Matthew 3:17, NKJV)

Notice—this affirmation came before the ministry, not after. The Father's love was not based on performance but on relationship. Jesus was chosen, loved, and affirmed simply because He was the Son.

And that same truth is yours. God does not wait for you to prove yourself before He calls you, His child. His choosing is not based on your record, but on His grace.

David: Anointed, Yet Hunted

David's story reveals the same pattern. When Samuel came to anoint Israel's next king, Jesse paraded his older sons before the prophet. But God rejected them all. Only when Samuel asked, "Are all the young men here?" did Jesse mention David—the forgotten shepherd in the fields (1 Samuel 16:11).

The one overlooked by his father was the one chosen by God. Samuel anointed David in the presence of his brothers, declaring God's favor upon him.

Yet soon after, David's life was not filled with royal glory but with rejection. King Saul, consumed with jealousy, hunted David across the wilderness. Though chosen and anointed, David was treated as an outlaw.

Still, God's choosing remained. And in time, the rejected shepherd became Israel's greatest king.

Chosen Even in Rejection

This is the mystery: being chosen by God does not mean you will be celebrated by men. Often, it means the opposite. The world may reject what God selects. But their rejection does not cancel His calling.

- Joseph was chosen yet thrown into a pit.

- David was chosen yet hunted.

- Jesus was chosen yet crucified.

God's choosing is not shaken by rejection—it is proven through it.

For You, Reader...

Rejection has left you feeling forsaken. Maybe you've believed the lie that if people reject you, God must have rejected you too. But hear this truth: You are chosen. You are beloved. You are not forsaken.

The voice of man may silence you, but the voice of God affirms you. And His voice is louder, stronger, and eternal.

Reflection

- Who has overlooked or rejected you in life?

- How has that made you doubt you are calling or worth?

- What would it mean to live secure in God's choosing rather than man's approval?

Prayer

Father, thank You that I am chosen and not forsaken. Thank You that, like Jesus, I am affirmed by Your voice, not man's. Thank You that, like David, I may be overlooked by people but never forgotten by You. Lord, root my identity in Your choosing. Help me to walk boldly in the assurance that I am loved, called, and secure in You. In Jesus' name, amen.

CHAPTER 11
WALKING IN PROPHETIC PURPOSE

Rejection may bruise your heart, but it cannot cancel God's plan. Betrayal may delay you, but it cannot deny what God has spoken. When God places a calling on your life, it will happen—not by man's approval, but by His sovereign hand.

The challenge for us is this: will we keep walking toward purpose, even when rejection tries to turn us back?

Jesus: Setting His Face Toward Jerusalem

As Jesus' ministry grew, so did the opposition. The Pharisees plotted against Him, the crowds turned away, and even His disciples misunderstood His mission. Yet none of this moved Him from His purpose.

Luke tells us:

"Now it came to pass, when the time had come for Him to be received

up, that He steadfastly set His face to go to Jerusalem. "
(Luke 9:51, NKJV)

Jesus knew what awaited Him in Jerusalem—betrayal, trial, rejection, the cross. Yet He walked forward, unmoved by fear, focused on fulfilling the Father's will.

Rejection could not stop Him. Betrayal could not derail Him. His prophetic purpose was stronger than the pain He endured.

Esther: Rising From Obscurity

Esther's story begins with rejection too. She was an orphan, raised in obscurity, with no royal background. By all human standards, she was unqualified to be queen. Yet God's hand was on her life.

When her people faced annihilation, Mordecai reminded her:

"Yet who knows whether you have come to the kingdom for such a time as this?"
(Esther 4:14, NKJV)

Esther could have stayed silent. Fear could have held her back. But she chose courage. She stepped into her calling, risking her life to stand before the king. And through her obedience, an entire nation was spared.

The orphan girl became a deliverer. The rejected one became the chosen vessel.

Prophetic Purpose Beyond Rejection

This is the lesson: rejection often positions us for prophetic purpose.

- Joseph's pit led him to Pharaoh's palace.

- Moses' wilderness led him to deliver Israel.

- Esther's obscurity led her to the throne.

- Jesus' rejection led Him to the cross—and through the cross, to resurrection.

God uses rejection as redirection. He turns pain into preparation. He transforms wounds into witness and calling into commission.

For You, Reader…

You are standing at a crossroads right now. You feel the weight of rejection, and the path ahead looks hard. But like Jesus, you must set your face toward your Jerusalem. Like Esther, you must rise up for such a time as this.

Your purpose is bigger than your pain. Your calling is stronger than your rejection. And your God is greater than the voices that oppose you.

Reflection

- What "Jerusalem" has God set before you that feels daunting or costly?

- Where has rejection tempted you to turn back instead of pressing forward?

- Can you trust that your pain is part of God's preparation for your prophetic purpose?

Prayer

Father, thank You that rejection cannot cancel my purpose. Thank You that, like Jesus, I can set my face toward what You have called me to, even when it is hard. Thank You that, like Esther, you have positioned me for such a time as this. Strengthen me, Lord, to walk in courage, to trust Your timing, and to fulfill the calling You have placed on my life. In Jesus' name, amen.

Chapter 12
Silence That Roars

Silence is not always weakness. In the hands of God, silence becomes a roar that shakes heaven and earth. When the world expects you to fight back, explain yourself, or collapse under pressure—but instead you stay still in God's strength—your silence speaks louder than a thousand words.

Jesus: Silence at the Cross

On the cross, Jesus bore the weight of sin, shame, and rejection. He had every right to call down angels, to demand justice, to prove His innocence. Yet He did not. Instead, He stayed in the Father's will.

The Gospels tell us that as He hung there, darkness covered the land, the earth quaked, and the veil of the temple tore in two (Matthew 27:45–51). Heaven and earth responded, even though Jesus said little.

His silence roared louder than His words. The Lamb's surrender shook the powers of hell, broke the grip of sin, and declared once for all: "It is finished."

The world saw defeat. But heaven heard victory.

Job: Silence in Suffering

Job, too, knew the roar of silence. Stripped of wealth, family, and health, he sat in ashes while friends accused him, and his wife urged him to curse God. Yet Job chose silence over bitterness.

The Bible says:

"In all this Job did not sin nor charge God with wrong."
(Job 1:22, NKJV)

His silence was not the absence of faith—it was the proof of it. Though he did not understand why he suffered, Job endured. And in the end, God restored him with double blessing (Job 42:10).

Job's silent endurance roared across generations as a testimony of faith under fire.

The Roar of a Life Surrendered

The silence of Jesus on the cross and the silence of Job in suffering both reveal this truth: silence surrendered to God is not emptiness—it is power. It declares:

- "My trust is in God, not in man."

- "My vindication comes from the Lord."

- "My pain is not the end of my story."

Your silence may not seem like much now. But in heaven, it is a roar. It is the sound of faith that refuses to quit. It is the echo of trust that shakes the enemy's hold.

For You, Reader…

Perhaps you have been misunderstood, betrayed, or rejected. Perhaps you have cried out and only silence returned. But let me tell you: God is not absent in your silence. He is present. And your silence in His presence is not weakness—it is strength.

Your silence is roaring louder than you know. It is testifying to unseen powers that you are still standing, still trusting, still chosen. And one day, like Job, you will see restoration. Like Jesus, you will see resurrection.

Reflection

- Where has silence been forced on you through rejection or betrayal?

- Can you see how your silence, endured in faith, might be roaring in heaven?

- What might God want to declare through your surrender?

Prayer

Father, thank You that silence is not the end—it is the beginning of a roar. Thank You for Jesus, who in His silence at the cross shook the heavens. Thank You for Job, whose endurance became a testimony for generations. Lord, take my silence, my pain, my surrender, and turn it into a roar that declares Your glory. May my life speak louder than words, testifying that I am Yours. In Jesus' name, amen.

CHAPTER 13
MY JOURNEY THROUGH IT ALL

As I have shared these pages, I have not written as an observer, but as one who has walked the valley of rejection myself. These words are not theory for me—they are scars that have been healed, tears that have been counted, prayers that have been answered in the silence.

When I was authoring my last book, I was facing some of the deepest rejection I had ever known. I felt the sting of betrayal from people I thought would stand with me. I felt the silence of friends who disappeared when I needed them most. The place I thought would bring me strength became the very place that brought me

And yet—it was in that season that the Lord met me in a deeper way. When the voices of man grew silent, His voice became clearer. When the approval of others was stripped away, I discovered the unshakable reality of His choosing. When doors closed in my face, I began to see the new ones He was opening.

I learned that rejection is not the end of the story—it is often the beginning of a new chapter in God's plan. I learned that silence, though painful, can roar with the testimony of trust. And I learned that wounds, once surrendered to God, become witnesses that others can lean on.

Through it all, I have come to understand that I am not defined by the rejection of men, but by the acceptance of God. I am not held back by betrayal but propelled forward by His purpose. I am not silenced by pain but strengthened to speak through the life that He continues to shape in me.

So, if you are reading this with fresh wounds or old scars, I want you to know I understand. I have been there. But more importantly, Jesus has been there too—and He is with you now.

My journey is still unfolding, but I no longer see rejection as a tombstone. I see it as a turning point. Every tear, every silence, every betrayal has been woven into the story of God's faithfulness in my life.

And if He can carry me through it all, He will carry you too.

It all began in 2015 when I found myself in a season of transition. I was in a relationship which, just six months in, I knew was wrong. I tried to give it a chance, but it was to no avail. At one point I even decided to move out and end it, but she begged me to stay, saying it would be different this time. But it wasn't any better.

It was during that time that God was working in me. I began seeking Him more earnestly, reading my Bible not as a Catholic—as I had been raised in a Catholic family far from God—but as a desperate child crying out to know my purpose in life.

One morning in March of 2015, I woke up, sat on the edge of the bed, and heard a voice inside of me say: "Pack your things and go." For some reason, I didn't even hesitate. I got up, packed my stuff, loaded my truck, and left while she was at work. I called a friend I was doing ministry work with and explained what had happened. He took me in for a short time.

It was then that things began to shift dramatically in me. I felt fire and wind on my head—something so real that I thought I was going crazy. I explained it to my friend, and he told me it was the Holy Spirit and that I had a calling on my life. As I read the scriptures, I come across the book of Act 2:3.

"Then there appeared to them divided tongues, as of fire, and one sat upon each of them."

Acts 2:3 Nkjv

I could feel the wind and the fire popping on my head, and I feel the heat of the fire, but I could not see it physically as I looked in the mirror but spiritually, I could feel it. I knew then I had to surrender my life totally to God.

From then on, it felt like hell broke loose. Even my friend turned against me, and I moved into my own place. I faced a lot of witchcraft attacks, spiritual attacks fighting with demons trying to kill me and to destroy my body. There was this night I will never forget, as I slept at night a demon come so powerful I could feel the wind of him rushing on me and he had a screwdriver in his had and he stabbed me on right side of my hip and I could feel the screwdriver right in my hip joint and he started to twist it to dislocate my hip joint and I could hear and feel my hip joint cracking. It was so painful as I was wrestling with him and at the same time praying Jesus, Jesus, and the third time i said Jesus it vanished.

I cried out to God, asking why this was happening. One night in my sleep He spoke a word to me: "Permeate." I didn't even know what it meant, so I looked it up in the dictionary. It means "to pass through." God was telling me not to run from these trials and tribulations but to go through them with Him. From then on, I stopped crying and started asking God to teach me His Word so I could know how to pray against the power of darkness and to know how to live righteous and holy. I even asked Him to find and show me my wife.

God gave me a deep hunger for His Word, all I did hence forth was studying His Word and I am still intrigued by it even til this day. And one night as I Was in my sleep, the Lord gave me a vision and in that vision I saw myself in a kitchen standing on the right side of a my wife, I could see her dark hair falling over her shoulders and I could only see her right side of her face for she was facing forward but I could see her skin tone on her face and her arms. And She was holding a child in her arms—a child with curly black hair, mixed in appearance. I have held onto that vision for ten years, and by God's grace I have stayed single and kept myself pure, compelled by the fear of God to live holy and righteous.

After that in the same vision the Holy Spirit snatched me and I could see myself flying passing the clouds and at some point I saw myself by a waterfall and in no time I found myself in a house setting in a corner of what seemed to be a living room and the Holy Spirit told me to watch what was happening in that house. As I opened my eyes and looked around the room, I saw a man and his family, as I observed what this man was doing, and it was not good at all, and I knew this man and his family. I understand exactly why the Holy Spirit wanted me to see that, and in no time, I separated myself from this man.

In 2017, I asked God where He would have me move, and He answered me in a dream: "Move to Tulsa, Oklahoma." I had no idea where Tulsa was, so I looked it up. I learned about the great revivals in its history, but also its dark side of racism and injustice. Honestly, it scared me, but I asked God when He wanted me to move, and He told me: "In a short season." That same month, my landlord told me to move out. I knew it was time.

I packed what I could fit in my car, gave away the rest, and drove to Tulsa. As I did not know anything there found an apostolic church online and used the address as my destination on my GPS. I arrived there one Saturday evening. Parking my car in the parking lot of the church, I started praying and I wept to God surrendering it all:"Not my will, but Yours be done." Now I knew I dead to self, it was no longer I living but Christ in me. As I prayed let it be so, let it be so, let it be son my Father in the name of Jesus Christ.

After that I went to find the cheapest motel, I could find and paid for a week, and the next day was Sunday. I attended the service at that church, and they welcomed me as the usher asked me if it were my first time at the church and he asked me where I was from as my accent could not hide my origin and I told him from Zambia in Africa. As the service was over, I noticed the church was 98% Caucasian and a mixture of black Americans and Latinos. During the week, I found a local library as was my custom to study the word of God and on Wednesday I attended the middle week service.

As two weeks passed one of the leaders in the church asked me what brought me to Tulsa.? I told him that God told me to move to Tulsa Oklahoma, and he asked me how I found out about the church and I told him I searched for apostolic and Pentecostal church, and your church came up so I got the address and that's how come to this church. Then he asked what I did for work and I told him that I did have a job at the moment but I'm looking for one but i have committed my life to study the word of God, then he asked me what Bible college am attending and I told him that I study by myself with the help of the Holy Spirit. This created suspicion about me from how he looked at me, and I could sense in the Spirit there were questions being asked about me with in the church. I could feel the tension when I attended services. I could see people's looks when I entered the church and chattering was going on about me.

As God would have it, one of those days I was at the library studying the word with all the materials I had spread on the table and one of the ladies at the church happened to come to the library and she saw me and came over to say hi. As we said hi to each other, she asked is the is what you do? And I said every day I come to study the word. She went and told the people at, and this created more tension with some pastors at church. I noticed a change in the demeanor towards me I could not understand why at that time. They started watching every step I take. They even had people watching me at the motel and at the library. It is like I was a threat to them. But I as usual would take it the Lord in prayer and the Lord gave understanding of what was going on.

It so happened that the founding pastor was considering retiring and I understood why the other pastors who were inline to replace him became so cold towards me because rumors were going around the church that maybe God sent me to that to take over the church and when ever they would preach they would preach threat at me saying they will make me park and send me on my and the world he would even mention about the way I dressed in a three piece suit as if I was a preacher.

But God encouraged me. One day at the library, an elderly woman approached me at the table I was studying the word, and she sat across from me. When she sat down, she asked me what book I was reading, and I said the book of John. Then she told me that her father's name was John, and her brothers name was John too, then She said to me the Lord told her exactly where to find me, to tell me that everything will be okay and not to worry about anything. It was like a heavy weight was lifted off my shoulders. We both wept as she spoke those words. That same week, during Sunday service, the founding pastor called me by name, at first, I thought he was calling another Peter in the church, but he pointed at me and told me to go in front so he would pray for me. He laid his hands on me and prayed for me in front of the congregation. It was God's confirmation: man may reject me, but He affirms me.

As Christmas approached, I did not feel like spending Christmas alone in the motel so I called and asked friends in Texas if I would spend Christmas with them and they graciously said yes so drove down to Texas. As I was there, I spent time in fasting and prayer asking God what he would have me to do since things at church were becoming tense. God gave me peace and spoke: "I was testing your obedience."

I eventually settled in Texas in 2018, found work as a caregiver, and later began attending a church in Denton. I knew in my spirit that God wanted to use that church for miracles, signs, and wonders, But the church was not ready for it even with undeniable proofs. But people were caught up in jealousy and evil and hatred towards me. Again, the sting of rejection was playing out just as the earlier church all because of titles and positions in the church. They started to connive against me lies were spread about me, plots were made against me, I was watched as if I was a criminal, all because I was a threat to them. It reminded me of Daniel 6—when leaders schemed against him out of envy.

I often asked God: "Are these people truly saved?" For how can someone say they love God yet hate their brother? Scripture says:

"If anyone says, 'I love God,' and hates his brother, he is a liar."
(1 John 4:20)

"The one who does not love does not know God, because God is love."
(1 John 4:8)

"Everyone who hates his brother is a murderer, and you know that no murderer has eternal life abiding in him."
(1 John 3:15)

Finally, a preacher openly declared from the pulpit that they had rejected me. I remembered Jesus' words:

"And whoever will not receive you nor hear you, when you depart from there, shake off the dust under your feet as a testimony against them."
(Mark 6:11)

So, I humbly called the senior pastor and told him my decision to leave the church, and I asked him to release me. Next day he texts me and released me. I forgave them, blessed them, and prayed for their prosperity.

Since then, I have faced the same treatment in other places. But I have learned that God has made me a stumbling block to some. It is not about me—it is about the calling and anointing He placed on me. I have never cared for titles or positions. If I can fulfill God's purpose without a title in front of my name, I am content.

Through it all, I am still silent before men but not before my Lord. My place is in the secret place, with the love of my soul—my darling Jesus Christ. I continue to trust Him for the vision of my wife He gave me ten years ago, and for the fulfillment of His purpose in my life.

Reflection

- Where in your life has rejection tested your obedience?

- Have you seen how God affirms you even when others reject you?

- Can you release those who hurt you and bless them as Jesus did?

Prayer

Father, thank You for walking with me through rejection, betrayal, and misunderstanding. Thank You for every word You have spoken and every vision You have given. I surrender the pain of my journey to You. Lord, help me forgive those who hurt me, and let my life be a testimony of Your faithfulness. I wait for the fulfillment of every promise You have spoken. In Jesus' name, amen.

When I look back, I see that my journey has been marked by rejection, betrayal, false accusations, and misunderstanding—but through it all, the Lord has been faithful. My scars are not signs of defeat, but testimonies of His grace.

Still Standing

""Blessed are the poor in spirit, for theirs is the kingdom of heaven. Blessed are those who mourn, for they shall be comforted. Blessed are the meek, for they shall inherit the earth. Blessed are those who hunger and thirst for righteousness, for they shall be filled. Blessed are the merciful, for they shall obtain mercy. Blessed are the pure in heart, for they shall see

God. Blessed are the peacemakers, for they shall be called sons of God. Blessed are those who are persecuted for righteousness' sake, for theirs is the kingdom of heaven. "Blessed are you when they revile and persecute you and say all kinds of evil against you falsely for My sake. Rejoice and be exceedingly glad, for great is your reward in heaven, for so they persecuted the prophets who were before you."

Over the years, I have faced misunderstanding, jealousy, and rejection from places I thought I would find love. Many times, I stayed silent—not out of weakness, but because my only refuge was in the presence of Jesus Christ. Am a quiet person, I do not talk much, and I would rather stay in the background, and I have noticed that were ever I go I attract attention not because seek it. I did ask the Lord why it is like that and the Lord answered and said because you are conspicuous.

"Also, He said to them, "Is a lamp brought to be put under a basket or under a bed? Is it not to be set on a lampstand?"

I have understood that what God has placed on my life has made me a stumbling block to many, especially those of the body of Christ.NOT because I sought positions or power, but because God's calling on my life intimidates religious people and those who live for titles. I have never cared for positions—only to fulfill the purpose of God.

And so, I continue forward, still single but holding onto the vision God gave me of my wife. Still misunderstood, but walking with the One who knows me fully. Still rejected by men but chosen by God.

Reflection

- How does my story resonate with your own?

- Can you begin to see your rejection not as the end, but as part of God's greater plan?

- What chapter might God be writing in your life through your present struggles?

Prayer

Father, thank You for carrying me through every season of rejection, silence, and betrayal. Thank You for turning pain into purpose and wounds into witness. Lord, as I close this journey, I pray for every reader holding this book. May they find comfort in knowing they are not alone. May they see that what man rejects, you embrace, and what man forsakes, you redeem. Carry them through, Lord, as You have carried me. In Jesus' name, amen.

CHAPTER 14
FAITH, THE PRINCIPAL THING

As this journey ends, I want to leave you with the foundation that makes everything else possible: faith.

The Bible says plainly:

"For we walk by faith, not by sight."
(2 Corinthians 5:7, NKJV)

"But without faith it is impossible to please Him, for he who comes to God must believe that He is, and that He is a rewarder of those who diligently seek Him."
(Hebrews 11:6, NKJV)

Rejection can shake us. Betrayal can wound us. Silence can test us. Circumstances can discourage us. But faith anchors us to the unchanging Word of God. Faith reminds us that His promises are true, even when our experiences say otherwise.

Faith in the Pages of Scripture

The whole story of redemption is written in the ink of faith.

- Abraham left his homeland, not knowing where he was going, but trusting the promise of a land and descendants as numerous as the stars.

- Joseph held onto his dreams through betrayal, slavery, and prison, believing God's purpose would prevail.

- Moses stood before Pharaoh and the Red Sea, believing that God's power was greater than Egypt's armies.

- David faced Goliath with a sling and a stone, trusting not in himself but in the God of Israel.

- The prophets spoke words they never saw fulfilled in their lifetime, yet believed God would bring them to pass.

- And Jesus endured the cross, despising its shame, because of the joy set before Him (Hebrews 12:2).

Faith is not wishful thinking. Faith is not denial of reality. Faith is confidence in the God who speaks and cannot lie. It is believing that His Word is greater than man's rejection, His promise stronger than your pain, and His purpose higher than you are understanding.

Why Faith Matters

Faith is the lens through which we see God's hand at work when others only see failure. Faith lifts our eyes above circumstances to the throne of heaven. Faith enables us to endure rejection, betrayal, and silence without losing hope.

Your rejection does not disqualify your faith—it refines it. Your scars do not destroy your faith—they testify to it. The silence of others does not weaken your faith—it strengthens your reliance on the One who speaks in whispers.

The enemy's goal in rejection is to destroy your faith. But God's purpose in allowing rejection is to deepen it.

For You, Reader...

If you take nothing else from this book, take this: Believe God.

- Believe Him when others reject you.

- Believe Him when you are misunderstood.

- Believe Him when the circumstances look impossible.

- Believe Him when His promises seem delayed.

Faith is the key that unlocks the promises of God. Faith is the victory that overcomes the world (1 John 5:4). Faith is the one thing the enemy cannot destroy, because it is rooted not in your strength, but in God's truth.

Reflection

- What situation in your life right now requires you to walk by faith and not by sight?

- Which promises of God have you struggled to keep believing?

- How can you strengthen your faith daily through prayer and the Word?

Prayer

Father, thank You for the gift of faith. Thank You that my life is not built on man's approval or my circumstances, but on Your eternal Word. Lord, increase my faith. Teach me to walk by faith and not by sight. Help me to believe Your promises even when everything around me says otherwise. May my faith please You, sustain me, and bring glory to Your name. In Jesus' name, amen.

Final Word to the Reader

My beloved friend,

As you close this book, I want to speak to your heart as one who has walked through rejection, betrayal, false accusation, and long seasons of silence. I know the sting of being misunderstood. I know what it feels like when those you thought would stand with you turn against you. Perhaps you do too.

But here is the truth I have come to know rejection is not the end—it is the beginning of God's elevation.

The enemy will use rejection, persecution, betrayal, and false accusations as weapons to break you. He wants you to believe you are forgotten, unworthy, and cast aside. But God uses these same weapons to shape you, refine you, and prepare you for His purpose. What man rejects, God selects. What wounds you, He heals and transforms into testimony. What silences you, He turns into the loudest declaration of His glory.

Joseph's betrayal carried him to the palace. David's rejection prepared him for the throne. Jesus' silence at the cross shook the earth and opened heaven. And so, it will be with you.

Every tear, every lonely night, every whisper of accusation—they are not wasted. They are being woven into the story of God's faithfulness in your life. Your silence is not emptiness—it is a roar in heaven. Your scars are not shame—they are proof that you survived and that God's hand is still on you.

So, lift your head. You are not forgotten. You are not forsaken. You are chosen, beloved, and destined for more than the enemy ever wanted you to believe. Walk by faith, not by sight. Hold fast to His promises. And let your silence speak louder than the lies of men—testifying to the goodness and glory of your Savior.

And now I want to pray for you:

Father, I lift every person who has read these words. Where there has been rejection, give them acceptance in You. Where there has been betrayal, give them peace. Where there has been silence, let them hear Your voice. May their scars become testimonies, their tears become seeds of joy, and their lives shine with Your glory. Lord, raise them up in faith, and let their silence speak louder than every lie of the enemy. In Jesus' name, amen.

With love in Christ,
Peter Lengwe

Promises of God for the Rejected but Chosen of God

When rejection, persecution, and false accusations come against you, hold fast to the eternal Word of God. These Scriptures remind you of your identity, your purpose, and God's unfailing promises.

God Knew You Before the Beginning

- "Before I formed you in the womb I knew you; before you were born, I sanctified you; I ordained you a prophet to the nations." – Jeremiah 1:5

- "Your eyes saw my substance, being yet unformed. And in Your book, they all were written, the days fashioned for me, when yet there were none of them." – Psalm 139:16

God Will Finish What He Started

- "Being confident of this very thing, that He who has begun a

good work in you will complete it until the day of Jesus Christ."
– Philippians 1:6

- "The Lord will perfect that which concerns me; Your mercy, O
Lord, endures forever; do not forsake the works of Your hands."
– Psalm 138:8

God's Plans Are for Good, Not Evil

- "For I know the thoughts that I think toward you, says the Lord,
thoughts of peace and not of evil, to give you a future and a
hope." – Jeremiah 29:11

- "And we know that all things work together for good to those
who love God, to those who are the called according to His
purpose." – Romans 8:28

God is Your Defender

- "No weapon formed against you shall prosper, and every tongue
which rises against you in judgment you shall condemn." – Isaiah
54:17

- "The Lord will fight for you, and you shall hold your peace." –
Exodus 14:14

- "When the enemy comes in like a flood, the Spirit of the Lord
will lift up a standard against him." – Isaiah 59:19

God Will Never Forsake You

- "When my father and my mother forsake me, then the Lord will
take care of me." – Psalm 27:10

- "Fear not, for I am with you; be not dismayed, for I am your God.
I will strengthen you, yes, I will help you, I will uphold you with
My righteous right hand." – Isaiah 41:10

- "For He Himself has said, 'I will never leave you nor forsake you.'" – Hebrews 13:5

You Are Chosen and Precious

- "The stone which the builders rejected has become the chief cornerstone." – Psalm 118:22

- "But you are a chosen generation, a royal priesthood, a holy nation, His own special people, that you may proclaim the praises of Him who called you out of darkness into His marvelous light." – 1 Peter 2:9

- "You did not choose Me, but I chose you and appointed you that you should go and bear fruit, and that your fruit should remain." – John 15:16

God's Love is Unshakable

- "The Lord has appeared of old to me, saying: 'Yes, I have loved you with an everlasting love; therefore, with lovingkindness I have drawn you.'" – Jeremiah 31:3

- "For I am persuaded that neither death nor life, nor angels nor principalities nor powers, nor things present nor things to come… shall be able to separate us from the love of God which is in Christ Jesus our Lord." – Romans 8:38–39

- "The Lord is near to those who have a broken heart and saves such as have a contrite spirit." – Psalm 34:18

Your Trials Will Become Testimonies

- "For our light affliction, which is but for a moment, is working for us a far more exceeding and eternal weight of glory." – 2 Corinthians 4:17

- "Blessed are those who are persecuted for righteousness' sake, for theirs is the kingdom of heaven." – Matthew 5:10

- "You meant evil against me; but God meant it for good, in order to bring it about as it is this day, to save many people alive." – Genesis 50:20

Declarations of Faith

- Chapter 1 – When Silence Speaks

- "God is speaking even in my silence. His presence is louder than the voices around me."

- Chapter 2 – The Ache of Betrayal

- "Betrayal will not break me. God turns every wound into a testimony of His love."

- Chapter 3 – The Hidden Battle of Identity

- "I am not defined by man's rejection. I am defined by God's choosing."

- Chapter 4 – Silent Strength

- "My strength is in God alone. I will stand firm even when I am silenced."

- Chapter 5 – The Cornerstone Rejected

- "What man rejects, God makes valuable. I am a living stone in His house."

- Chapter 6 – The Voice in the Silence

- "I will listen for God's whisper. His still, small voice leads me in every season."

- Chapter 7 – What Man Rejects, God Selects

- "God's hand is on me. What others reject, He has chosen for His glory."

- Chapter 8 – Healing the Wounds of Church Hurt

- "The wounds from people will not define my walk. Christ is my healer and defender."

- Chapter 9 – From Wounds to Witness

- "My scars are not shame. They are testimonies of God's grace and healing power."

- Chapter 10 – Chosen, Not Forsaken

- "I am chosen, loved, and never forsaken. God's call on my life cannot be cancelled."

- Chapter 11 – Walking in Prophetic Purpose

- "I will set my face toward God's will. His purpose will prevail in my life."

- Chapter 12 – Silence That Roars

- "My silence in faith is not weakness. It roars in heaven and shakes the enemy."

- Chapter 13 – My Journey Through It All

- "Every rejection I faced has prepared me. My journey is proof of God's faithfulness."

- Chapter 14 – Faith, the Principal Thing

- "I will walk by faith and not by sight. My faith pleases God and secures my victory."

www.ingramcontent.com/pod-product-compliance
Lightning Source LLC
Chambersburg PA
CBHW022000170726
47994CB00021B/1342